by Noah Leatherland

Minneapolis, Minnesota

Credits
Images are courtesy of Shutterstock.com. With thanks to Getty Images, Thinkstock Photo, and iStockphoto. Recurring Images – vectorplus. Cover – Sonechko57, Om Yos, baldezh, FoxGrafy, Buravleva stock, fox_workshop, stockvit. 4–5 – XOOXO, stockvit, Tartila. 6–7 – W. Scott McGill, Alex Coan, simplevect, Zhenyakot, Poozeum, CC BY-SA 4.0 <https://creativecommons.org/licenses/by-sa/4.0>, via Wikimedia Commons. 8–9 – Quarta, NotionPic, spline_x, NiRain, nikiteev_konstantin, Monory. 10–11 – Elena11, yusufdemirci, Nazarii_Neshcherenskyi, NASA, Public domain, via Wikimedia Commons. 12–13 – nevio, Magicleaf, NPavel. 14–15 – Rosa Jay, Agussetiawan99, traction, Pong Wira, Anatolir. 16–17 – Angel DiBilio, J.J. Gouin, Chase D'animulls, robuart, Kamla S, Ishor gurung, Elena Istomina. 18–19 – Susan Flashman, Mandy Creighton, Picture Partners, Alan Tunnicliffe, Ondrej Prosicky, Magura. 20–21 – Karel Cerny, Sensvector, WinWin artlab, AKKHARAT JARUSILAWONG, Thampitakkull Jakkree. 22–23 – Jane Rix, koblizeek, MaryValery, chetanya kumar suman, Scharfsinn, Nsit. 24–25 – Lazy_Bear, Taphat Wangsereekul, Alfmaler, Ksenia Ragozina, Derariad. 26–27 – Cornell University Library, Public domain, via Wikimedia Commons, Punch Magazine, Public domain, via Wikimedia Commons, Martial Red, billedfab, StockSmartStart. 28–29 – Pascale Gueret, Andrew Sutton. 30 – ShadowBird.

Bearport Publishing Company Product Development Team
President: Jen Jenson; Director of Product Development: Spencer Brinker; Managing Editor: Allison Juda; Associate Editor: Naomi Reich; Associate Editor: Tiana Tran; Art Director: Colin O'Dea; Designer: Kim Jones; Designer: Kayla Eggert; Product Development Assistant: Owen Hamlin

Library of Congress Cataloging-in-Publication Data is available at www.loc.gov or upon request from the publisher.

ISBN: 979-8-89232-067-2 (hardcover)
ISBN: 979-8-89232-541-7 (paperback)
ISBN: 979-8-89232-200-3 (ebook)

© 2025 BookLife Publishing
This edition is published by arrangement with BookLife Publishing.

North American adaptations © 2025 Bearport Publishing Company. All rights reserved. No part of this publication may be reproduced in whole or in part, stored in any retrieval system, or transmitted in any form or by any means, electronic, mechanical, photocopying, recording, or otherwise, without written permission from the publisher. Bearport Publishing is a division of Chrysalis Education Group.

For more information, write to Bearport Publishing, 5357 Penn Avenue South, Minneapolis, MN 55419.

CONTENTS

Insane, Wacky Poop............4

Dinosaur Poop 6

Pricey Poop.............8

Poops in Space 10

Poop Fight 12

Poop Pretenders..........14

Poop Shooters............16

Weird Poop 18

A Drink of Poop 20

Powered by Poop 22

Poop Paper 24

The Great Stink of 1858...........26

The Biggest Poopers 28

Plug Your Nose! 30

Glossary 31

Index..........32

Read More 32

Learn More Online..........32

INSANE, WACKY POOP

Everybody poops. Doo-doo can come in different shapes and sizes.

AFTER WE EAT, OUR FOOD GOES THROUGH OUR BODIES AND DOWN THE TOILET.

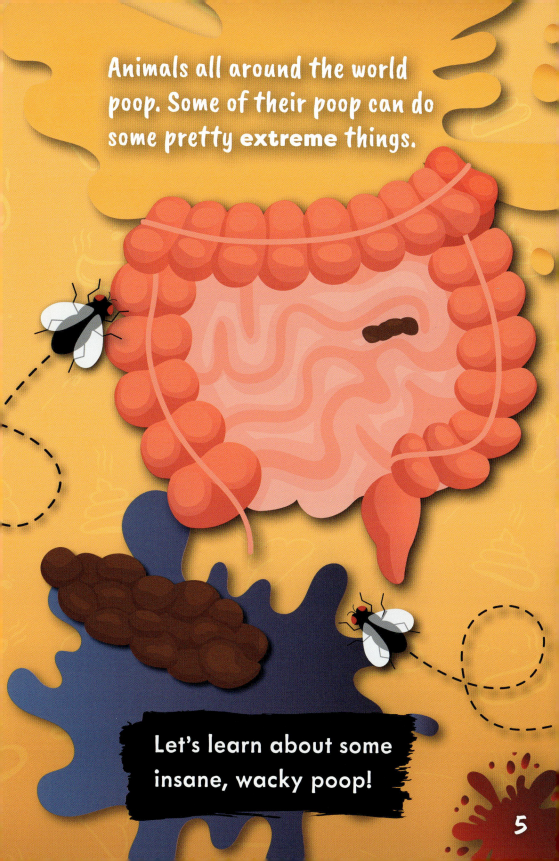

DINOSAUR POOP

Millions of years ago, dinosaurs lived on Earth. Some of their poop has lasted as long as their bones!

A COPROLITE

Scientists have dug up rocky balls of **fossilized** poop called coprolites (KAH-proh-litez).

The largest coprolite came from a **carnivore**. This fossil poop is around 27 inches (67 cm) long.

27 INCHES? THAT'S AS LONG AS A TENNIS RACKET!

One man has more than 1,000 rocky pieces of fossilized poo. His is the biggest coprolite collection in the world.

PRICEY POOP

What would you pay for poop? People have shelled out lots of money for large piles of whale poo.

AMBERGRIS

Some whale poop is known as ambergris (AM-bur-griss). It is often used in perfumes.

Scientists have found that human poop has tiny amounts of metals, such as silver and gold, inside.

FOLLOW THE SMELL TO GOLD!

Some scientists have even started searching sewers for poop with gold in it!

POOPS IN SPACE

Astronauts in space need to poop, too. But where does it all go?

Astronauts put their poop into bags. There are 96 bags of astronaut waste on the moon.

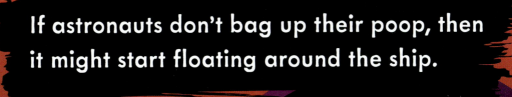

If astronauts don't bag up their poop, then it might start floating around the ship.

DURING THE APOLLO 10 SPACE MISSION, POOP FLOATED AROUND THE SHIP.

DO NOT MAKE A WISH ON A SHOOTING POOP.

Sometimes, astronaut poop falling from space toward Earth looks like a shooting star.

11

POOP FIGHT

In the past, people used the brown stuff as weapons in wars.

DON'T WORRY, THAT'S JUST MUD.

In ancient times, poop was put onto the tips of arrows. Being hit by one of these smelly arrows could make someone very sick.

POOP PRETENDERS

Some animals stay safe by . . . looking like poop!

It's easy to see how the bird poop frog got its name. It tucks its legs in to look like brown and white bird droppings.

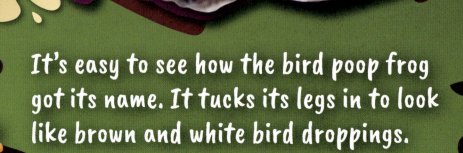

A giant swallowtail caterpillar looks like a long poop. This keeps hungry birds from eating the crawling critter.

The bird-dung crab spider not only looks like poop, but also makes itself smell like poop! The spider's **prey** follows the stinky smell and gets caught in its web.

POOP SHOOTERS

Some creatures are not shy about throwing their poop all over the place.

WATCH OUT!

CATERPILLAR POOP

Caterpillars can shoot their poop more than 3 feet (1 m) away.

Penguins get their poop out of their nests to keep their homes clean. They can shoot poop at speeds of 5 miles per hour (8 kph).

WE'RE COOL.

Turkey vultures shoot their poop . . . on themselves! This helps them stay cool.

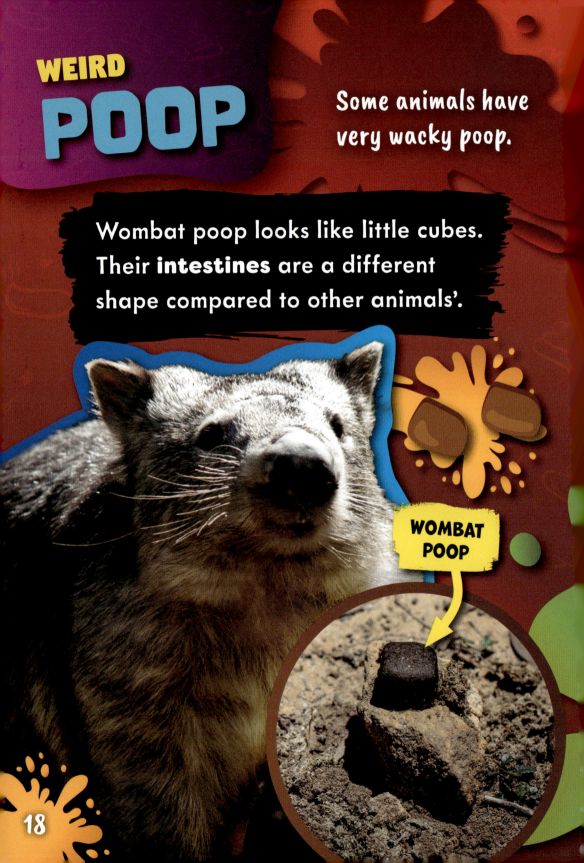

WEIRD POOP

Some animals have very wacky poop.

Wombat poop looks like little cubes. Their **intestines** are a different shape compared to other animals'.

WOMBAT POOP

Owls cannot poop out everything they eat. Instead, they cough up small, hard balls. The balls have the fur and bones of their prey inside.

CAN YOU SEE THE FUR AND BONES?

Capybaras have two types of poop. One type is waste. The other is soft and green. It is eaten by other capybaras.

A DRINK OF POOP

Would you drink something with poop in it? What do you think it would taste like?

As its name suggests, panda dung tea is made from giant panda droppings. It is one of the most expensive teas in the world.

People feed civets coffee cherries.

COFFEE CHERRIES

CIVET POOP

After eating the cherries, civets poop out balls of coffee beans. This poop is then used to make civet coffee.

POWERED BY POOP

Another thing poop is used for is **fuel**.

In Norway, some houses are heated by warm **sewage**. Machines suck the heat away from the poopy mix. Then, they pump the heat into the houses.

Cow droppings are used to make dung cakes. They are burned as fuel to heat ovens.

Some car engines run on the gas from human poop.

DUNG EAT THESE CAKES!

POOP POWER!

POOP PAPER

Did you know most people did not have toilet paper until 1857?

THAT'S NEARLY 100 YEARS OF PRICKLY WIPES!

Those that did were in for a sharp surprise. Back then, toilet paper had **splinters** in it. It wasn't until the 1930s that softer paper was first made.

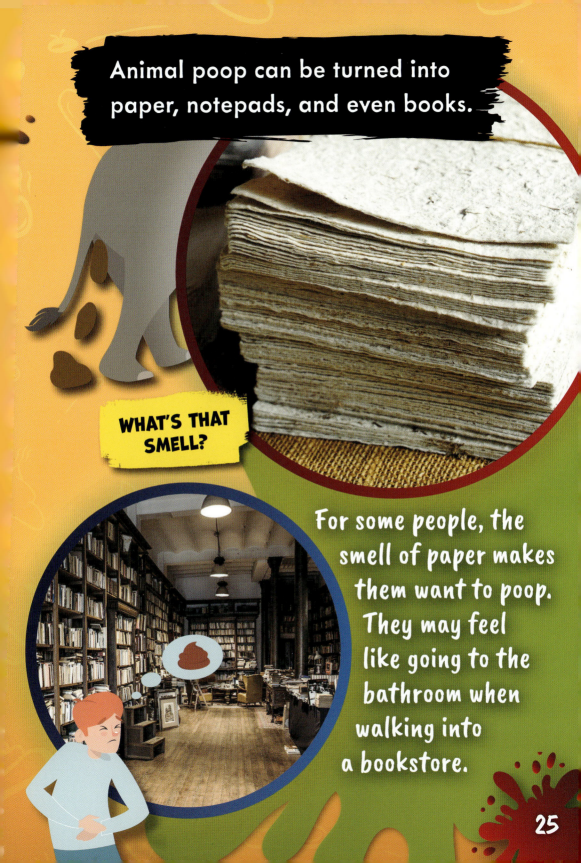

Animal poop can be turned into paper, notepads, and even books.

WHAT'S THAT SMELL?

For some people, the smell of paper makes them want to poop. They may feel like going to the bathroom when walking into a bookstore.

THE GREAT STINK of 1858

In London, sewage used to be dumped into the River Thames. This led to the Great Stink of 1858.

The summer of 1858 was very hot. It made the poop-filled river stink even more.

Stories say the smell was so bad that it caused people to throw up and faint.

SOME PEOPLE THOUGHT THE STINKY SMELL COULD EVEN KILL YOU.

Queen Victoria had to stop a boat trip because of the smell.

THE BIGGEST POOPERS

Some animals poop more than others.

WOULD YOU LIKE A PIECE OF BAM-POO?

Giant pandas spend more than 10 hours a day chowing down on bamboo. They poop around 40 times a day.

The largest animals on Earth are blue whales. It's no surprise that a big animal also has a big poop!

Blue whales let out 52 gallons (200 liters) of poop at once. Their poop helps feed other sea life.

PLUG YOUR NOSE!

From stinky weapons to smelly coffee, poop can make some weird things. That's what makes it extreme!

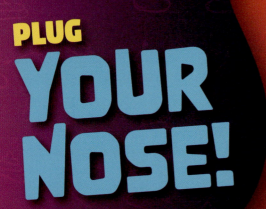

The next time you are sitting on the toilet, think about all the wacky stuff that poop can do.

GLOSSARY

astronauts people who go to space

carnivore an animal that eats only meat

extreme at the highest level with an element of risk

fossilized turned into a fossil

fuel to give energy or power to something

intestines the long, tube-shaped parts inside an animal's body where food is turned into useful fuel and waste

prey animals that are hunted by other animals for food

sewage solid and liquid waste from humans that goes down drains

splinters small, sharp pieces of wood

INDEX

astronauts	10–11	paper	24–25
Apollo 10	11	penguins	17
capybaras	19	perfume	8
caterpillars	15–16	tea	20
coffee	21, 30	whales	8, 29
pandas	20, 28	wombats	18

READ MORE

Murray, Laura K. *Why Do We Need Poop? (Nature We Need).* North Mankato, MN: Capstone, 2024.

Wilson, Libby. *Poop-Eating Animals (Weird Animal Diets).* Lake Elmo, MN: Focus Readers, 2022.

LEARN MORE ONLINE

1. Go to **www.factsurfer.com** or scan the QR code below.
2. Enter "**Poop Facts**" into the search box.
3. Click on the cover of this book to see a list of websites.